AF430841

PRAISE FOR LEARNING TO HOLD

Winner of the Wandering Aengus Press Editors' Award

In Jed Myers' beautiful and bracing collection, *Learning to Hold,* we are invited to consider the trauma of war, genocide, and the Holocaust, how "What stories aren't told are lived" and "Memories course the umbilicus." Myers, situating himself as grandson, son, nephew, and father, dwells on the ways "murder gets into what's grown," while reveling in nature's increasingly precious splendor. Despite the near-constant backbeat of the human predilection for strife, Myers revels in small moments of gratitude, reminding us "To stop / and honor the battered heads of the rushes," and that "maples and firs … are never toppled to ground / till they're ancestor old." In these rhymical and reverential poems, ancestors sputter and flicker like guiding spirits. Fervent and musical, these are the poems I want to reach for as we "remain mingled / in our mother's breath."
—Martha Silano, author of *Reckless Lovely* and *Gravity Assist*

Jed Myers' poetic power is the gale force that blows through the pages of *Learning to Hold,* as this poetry collection wrestles to grasp the whole of humanity's complexity and brutality. A boy's childhood begins as "memories course the umbilicus," and the legacy of family "history held in raised hands, winces, / flinches, and those strange-lit dreams" gives way to a larger landscape of the broken and chaotic world, where "dreams find too much to hold." But these are not dreamy poems. These poems slip in on gentle breezes but leave the reader wind-slapped, awakened in body and spirit. We feel these poems and trust the poet's urging to "get out and love the world, take the road/west, cross the known's edge, and trust/it isn't all war zone, this flesh."
—Heidi Seaborn, author of *An Insomniac's Slumber Party with Marilyn Monroe* and *Give a Girl Chaos*

Learning to Hold is a breathtaking collection that can be best described in Myers' own powerful words as "History held in raised hands, winces, / flinches, and those strange-lit dreams." These poems take us on a journey, from the trauma endured by the poet's ancestors in Eastern Europe through their flight across the water and into the present moment of delving into the ways where we come from haunts wherever we are. Myers interweaves his own sensory experience with his family's: in "Her Winter Borscht," his grandmother "… is my senses' tie to where / I'm from." Myers leaves us almost tasting the red of old-country beets and the violence it took to give them their color: "Still, the murder gets into what's grown / in this ground too. The roots all know." It is a collection that acknowledges profound, continual loss, "*Someone's* gone. Sunset's own wings / open to the edge of the world…" and yet the poems rise out from despair with perseverance, or dare I even say hope, reminding us, "You'll go on."
—Julia Kolchinsky Dasbach, author of *The Many Names for Mother* and *40 WEEKS*

How does one learn to hold steady in a world at odds with the human need for stability, peace, and empathy? In Jed Myers' collection *Learning to Hold*, this eternal question is explored. From moments of holding one's own child to the realization that "gravity grounds us all in its democratic hold," these poems reflect deeply on truths ranging from the brutality of war and racism to the wild grace in nature, dreams and memory. This work offers us its steadying hold in our whirlwind of longing, love, and loss.
—Tina Schumann, author of *Praising the Paradox* and *Requiem: A Patrimony of Fugues*

LEARNING TO HOLD

LEARNING TO HOLD

poems

Jed Myers

Wandering Aengus Press
Eastsound, WA

First Edition.
Published by Wandering Aengus Press

Poetry
ISBN: 979-8-218-29863-0
Printed in the United States of America.
Author Photo: Rosanne Olson
Cover Photo: Wyxina Tresse on Unsplash
Book Design: Jill McCabe Johnson

Wandering Aengus Press
PO Box 334 Eastsound, WA 98245
wanderingaenguspress.com

Wandering Aengus Press is dedicated to publishing works to enrich lives and make the world a better place.

This book is dedicated to my brother, Ford,
who's offered more encouragement than anyone.

CONTENTS

…the night sky takes no credit
for the moon, but continues to hold it…

—from the poem "So Much Happiness"
by Naomi Shihab Nye

I

RAIN'S MEMORY

> The blue flowers
> came up through the grass like the grass remembering.

> —from the poem "Siberian"
> by Jill Osier

Water-Lens

I hold you in a place behind
my thoughts a circle of tent cloths

they lift to sweeps of wind
it's the time-wind of course

and the face you wear there isn't
skin but memory it changes

shade and wavers to the bend
of my heart-eye's water-lens

and how else would I hold you
at this distance in our wanderings

WORD OF OUR CROSSING

I picture the gone villages, wooden
houses in small fenced herds.

In the cold cities, ghetto walk-ups
crowded over coal furnaces.

And before, tents amid flocks
in the valleys between dry hills.

And before, our shining dark shoulders
in starlight our first prayer shawls.

What stories aren't told are lived,
staged by our hearts and limbs.

History held in raised hands, winces,
flinches, and those strange-lit dreams.

A firstborn leaves, love's nails at his neck
long past the last look back.

And a little one's stock-still in a trunk
while shouts ensue at the gate.

A sister turns out to be the best liar.
It helps she likes the guard's boots.

We, the not-killed, are not released.
Memories course the umbilicus.

Snakes I'd never seen hissed me awake.
I knew the smell of charred beams.

And of our crossing, not a word.
Not one of our former names.

But a burn under my skin as the Syrian
kid finds my eyes through the screen.

Her Winter Borscht

It was murder, much as love, drove them
west, pressed them off the loam

where their dead's bones were left. Murder
in its dark red flamboyant cursive

wrote its recipe in those beds—charred
marrow, ash of prayer-book, hate-crushed

muscle, dread's sour salts, what all
the roots could savor, what beets

and apples would absorb, what lambs
and goats would grind to milk and meat—

it took murder's horseback swords
and torches just to sweep them off,

to leave the blossoms to the bees, the beet tops
to dusk's rabbits and night's voles.

Now it's dawn, and blinking out my window
on the leafy greens we've nursed, the staked

tomatoes and sprawled zucchini stalks,
there's a hint of her again, most soothing

scent in that bright kitchen where she builds
the broth, chops deep-red roots to matchsticks,

shreds the cabbage, hums a village
song…she is my senses' tie to where

I'm from, the girl of four she was come
by foot, cart, ship's deck to a smoking

riot of asylum, itself a stolen
garden, shackle-worked, gun-gated,

sharecropped, drilled and mined to stoke
its fired lungs. And this girl thrives,

heartbeat like mine will be, kill-quickened.
I see her at the butcher shop, hear that

endangered language on her lips. She knows
the lamb's blessed before the neck's slit, sure

each creature's prayed-for as its blood's let,
blade so fine it's hardly felt. She trusts

the butcher hangs his painted apron
on its hook before the sun sets

on what they call here Friday night,
and that he then bows his head in praise of all

creation. Which does not set things right.
But will let my grandmother stir

her love in with the murder, brisket
in her sweet-and-sour winter-garden stew,

her lineage of wariness and hope consigned
to my insides. And I work on leaving

all the kill I can out of the root soup
I cook for my little ones—there,

the leaves shine in the new sun. I'll go
wet those beds down while the light's low.

Still, the murder gets into what's grown
in this ground too. The roots all know.

Rain's Memory

It's dark out and I can hear the rain
through an open window, nothing to see
but a few lights haloed in the blur.

The downpour shakes a deep whisper
out of the trees. It could be the sea,
or wind through thick scrub on a bluff.

Could be the sound of time crashing
against life's reef, what we first heard

as blood coursed the new snail shells
of our inner ears. And I remember

my grandmother's bed, her windows
wide on a row of sycamores, a summer
shower—how the leaves roared

lulled me, that noise of the world
the rush and sizzle of surf, a water god's
or a sky god's hand brushing the earth,

a throng cheering its heroes home,
a radio on with no station. I'd float

that sonic ocean on my pillowed raft,
the fighting would go on downstairs,

my bellowing grandfather might strike
my aunt to the kitchen floor, and again
my father, called to the impossible

rescue, his black Buick growling
its harnessed explosions, would pull in
under the mottled boughs. It's all there

in the rain even now. I'm at the sill,
drifting once more to the harsh music,

fusion of countless staccato blows,
the pummeled leaves lifting our wounds.

Name I've Never Heard

It must've been hard to leave. For all
the burnings, stink of steam off char
in the rain, black posts and stubs of beams
like the attackers' haphazard crucifix

mementos; for all the storm-soaked hillside
eroding right off the beets, cabbage heads'
pale roots exposed; for all the cold
crystallizing its half the yield, panes glazed

whole winters of nights, demons composed
of moonlight; for all the hacking sick
keeping us from our dreams, the dead's silence
shaking us in the dark awake; for all the stark

ovals of blood on the snow, blood of the slow
to escape horse-high swords; for all the small
invasive creatures' names we were called;
for all the gunmetal stares—it must have been

hard to leave. My great-grandfather must've
believed there was that America where some
sailed, had written, sworn they had opened
their shops on wide streets in Philadelphia,

Brooklyn, little ones running home
from public schools speaking English. It would
be hard to swallow such blessings, to lose
the blood's old insistence on its separateness.

My great-grandfather left his name behind him
somewhere on a long mud road, or gave it
up to the wind as he waited to board
his ship, or dropped it in white-laced swells

one night from the rail where other men tapped
ash from the tips of cigars. Or when
he spoke his terrified hopes to the clerk
through the grate, said an American name,

and a name I've never heard went dead.

GAVEL

A question, a *when*, in that train-coach-narrow
living room, at our creaky dining room
table, in our tiny galley kitchen—

a *when again*, in those quiets between
our mother's eruptions. We knew there would be
another tearing at love's strained tendons,

but no words for it on any tongue's tip—
no, tongues held in our dread's silencing
grip. As though we were caught in a hard surf's

rush—sure we could drown if
we opened our mouths too much. So we wouldn't
inhale deep, not even to sing

the trouble's name, if we knew it. Which wouldn't
save us. It was about safety but not
about Russian missiles aimed from that island

outlined on the nightly news. Deathly sleeping
sickness mosquitoes might pass? The polio
licked off a friend's red popsicle? No,

there'd be no reporting outside our skin
for these blasts, or for apprehension's current
our limbs dreams thoughts shivered in

each moment, even through the long troughs
between the last and the next crests to crash
against us, her voice a howl-and-screech wind

of memories we'd never see but which were meant
to sudden us. What, an enraged god's sentencing,
or our inoculations for sensing

the blow, the galloping in the earth, the torch gang
again out of nowhere, that ever-raised gavel
we'd damn well know is about to land?

A Piece of String

Our brick row house, I never saw it
as narrow. Wasn't it wide as a truck?
And wasn't I, little one, giant
lord of that crumbling alley out back?

Didn't I shadow those battered valleys,
crouched to watch life pressing out
through the cracks, the grass tufts
my post-nuclear ferns, the dandelions

a new order's sunflowers? Ants, alien
or ally hordes. And over my ruins,
rising above the laundry-room door,
our fired-clay fortress, wasn't it

broad as Godzilla's paw? Where I lost
my warriors in the cement's fissures,
there sprouted elegant bluish blooms,
banners better than headstone pebbles.

Remember the old question How long
is a piece of string? How long
did my brother and I fly on our bikes
off the end of that lumber-scrap ramp

propped on a rock stolen from our own
mother's garden? It will be forever
unclocked. And how long till we drove
back down Parma Road and marveled,

our first home, so small and broken?
We'd been the insects on that tract
some lords in their clouds had mapped
paved and traded. Then we'd migrated,

across City Line for the schools. Times
I still want streets to split open, vines
sprung from the freed roots, sudden
stems like fat green anacondas, leaves

spread fast-as-dream and glinty
as executioners' blades over our heads,
the sky ready to be my memorial
petal, no stone to carve years in.

Through the Blows

I've come out in a hard slant rain,
down into the ravine, and planted

my soles in the creek bed's mud
till the wet cold's inside my bones,

to learn, from where the roots hide,
how the maples and firs can stand

the years of storms, how they lean
in give with the wind, hold firm,

bear the fallen clouds in their limbs
and are never toppled to ground

till they're ancestor old. I'll need
some human kind of rootedness

to live through the blows to come,
to not have my hope thrown down.

Sketch for a Counter-Manifesto

Once the St. Asaph's kids had thrown a few
Stones, enough of those *Christ-Killer*
And *Dirty Jew* darts, and seen the blood
Start on Elliott's head, they turned
And biked back to their neighborhood.

We rode up after them, pedaled fast
Like avenging horsemen, hooves splashing
The late-summer low river of Conshohocken
Avenue, natural divide between lands.

Crossing out of one brick-row-house realm
Into another, from curbside sycamores
To under those broadleaf maples, our Parma
Road turning to their 46th Street,

We were met by a heavyset sentinel
In curlers and robe, having a cigarette
Out on her landing. We felt her eyes
Find us and narrow to cast their time-slowing
Net. Down through the smoke of her breath,

To the beat of the back of the fist she held
Next to her scowl, fell the few words
She meant for us kids, the invaders
We were, brood of Lord-murderers, takers
Of her father's and sons' paid work…

Hitler shoulda finished his job…
Struck our faces our jackets and pants
And burned on through skin bone and innards,
Condemners' acid, bullets of nothing
But bitterness, hurt's blind inheritance.

We turned back to our homes, riddled
With new tunnels of world. Not one of us
Told. None of us spoke it. Now I am
Old. I see the curse-holes in all souls.

PRACTICING THE DRILL

—for all the conscripts

Boy's bright summer morning. So far
no final flash. Flesh still on the bone,
no package from Khrushchev whistling
down a last few bewildering seconds
till our eyes melt on our skeletons—no

burgeoning roar for an instant before
the ears' tiny moving parts splatter. Yet.
Chirps from the juniper hedge, a yip
off the new people's porch, buzz
of a twin-prop pulling for the sky's edge—no

cause a soul could see why I hold
my stemmy frame so straight and still
here on the concrete landing out front
of our little house, a real-enough-looking
rifle slanted across my chest—no

sense in it but that I must practice
the drill in the pamphlet. Two counts more
to *Right shoulder, arms!* I squint dead
ahead where sun flares the trees. I'll go
when I'm called. What could I say—no?

A Few Wars

They're reaching out to us with their guns.
They must want to make a difference

to someone—it's us they hail now
as dark super-figures, our values high
on the far side of zero. That's how much

I meant to young Chipper Miller. He had to
shove me. To hurl real stones.

He was reaching out too. And that stocky
guy who grew out of the night with a knife
in his hand as I turned from the cash machine.

By his ardent grin, I believed
it was more than money he needed—

me as a stand-in, understudy
for his cult-classic role, *Damn Little
Shithead*, aka *That Asshole Kid*....

Down the corridor of my dread
he stepped closer like a young soldier

through a farmer's front door. I remember
my friend, combat vet back from the war
a few wars back. Names he called himself,

the headaches, the shakes. He confessed—
shooting all the villagers was better than sex.

Having First Heard of the Ivory-Billed Woodpecker on its Being Pronounced Extinct

On the 20th Avenue Bridge, a memory
or flight of imagining: I hear myself
saying *Home* through my spread fingers

sweeping the green deciduous woods
of the ravine. I've got the kid scooped up
in my other arm. He bangs the rail

with the pudgy hand not tugging
my ear. Can he feel our height above
creek bed with his gut sense for falls?

His hoot sounds more like inspiration
for flight, like he might bolt from my grip
or slip free from the nest of his flesh

to rise like the weightless soul he could be
for all I know, out over the canopy
into unfenced expanse now that he sees

where he's from, the horizon cumuli
calling to him like the mountains of home.
Is there music? He's cooing to something.

All I hear is a plane's waning drone
fading south. And those scattered cries
from the branches, sources I can't name

for all my years—winged forms
who could be disappeared before this one
lifts from my arms to find home.

THE ROAD WEST

I left my kid brother standing alone
in the middle of our mother's living room
antique museum. I left him

flanked by the twin stone poodles
guarding the hearth. He held still for it,
lips like a dash between classified clauses,

eyes on the distance where I'd disappear,
and to one side the stuffed great white
chair that would swallow Dad while he died,

to the other the chartreuse and burgundy
stripes of the loveseat where no one sat
until there were funeral guests. I left

my brother there to be the one
satellite orbiting the gold crown
Dr. Goldman had set in Mom's mouth

back in that molten era when she hacked
smoke into the oatmeal she cooked us
for breakfast. I left my brother

hung with our father's worsted jackets
and camel-hair coats—left him to wear
the bequeathed tassel loafers I wouldn't

even if my feet were long enough. No,
I left him before all that, slipped
off in the mud of the creek to hunt newts

under the tall maples and mountain ash
between the cemetery and the abandoned
tracks—no, earlier still,

back when Mom whispered *This one's mine*
to herself as my brother was handed
fresh-toweled-off from the blood-wet of birth

into her arms, while Dad the courier
shuttled me over to *his* mother's house
in the flickering shade of sycamores. Yes,

I'd begun my departure before
they brought him home and Mom locked him
behind his bedroom door to keep him

secure from Cain—such the divisions
in the dark of Mom's heart, where I left him
in charge. And one of us had to

get out and love the world, take the road
west, cross the known's edge, and trust
it isn't all war zone, this flesh.

Empathy's Shadow

This clear late-fall afternoon, crows
gambol on whipping escalators of wind

off the lake. Sharp silhouettes fling
themselves from the trees to the heights,

only to be flipped by blasts of air, dropped
back to the fray of branches. No,

it's more—I see the crows play-
harass each other. They even gang up

a few against one, as on an eagle
who's flown too near a nest of their young.

Fending off an assault, a flyer
fails to adjust wings fast to a gust

and plummets. This game, seems they love it.
A bird hounded from the sky soars

on the next attack. How good it felt
to taunt the new day's targeted kid

along with the rest in our pack. Not me
again. It'd be Barry Lipton

spin-falling like a torn-off leaf
to scuff away on the mud. He'd disappear

into a row house like mine. Those times
I did secretly fear one of us

might make a life of hurting. After all that
curse and cringe. And given a crow

may also hold some self-sense, might it
ever, after one pointed jab

too many, unhinge talon and beak
to slash through another's skin to bone?

Knowing, as we do, how to get back.
Up on those buffeting blue ramps, dark

blades overlap as they loop and veer.
I linger to watch the crows clash, as if

I'll catch when one bloodies its own.

Nearing the After

There's time. Mom's losing
blood in her urine, it might be
a malignant erosion, but we spoke
last night on the phone, and she laughed
recalling her first dances with Dad—

laughed hard enough she coughed, and I thought
she'll crack a rib like that, hard enough
I imagined Dad could hear as he strolled
the unmowed grass between the rows of old
stones out at Har Jehuda—laughed

to remember how boyish and brash
he was, how hard she fell and never turned
back though his folks made of her life
a living hell. She said that and laughed.
There's time. Though she never forgives him

and secretly never herself, she can tell
I keep dulling the blade for her
with my listening. And she hears
a little each call about the kids—Taiwan,
Tarot, piano—I know it salves

the persistent fissures of her bitterness
some. And we both know, the after,
whether it comes in the form of fog
or agonal storm, will lift and we won't
find her, sky as our witness.

I Picture Him Driving

My father never said lonely. He'd say *Let's go to Alfredo's*. Soon
as he'd collapsed in the living room chair home from work. We'd see
how beat he was. He'd talk through his yawns,

then he'd thrust himself forward and push up off the chair's arms, go
wrestle his coat back on, and we'd follow him out the front door
to the car. He would drive

over the limit, slow down for stop signs or rights on red, and pull
a quick left through a brief gap in City Line's oncoming traffic
to land us in Alfredo's lot. He said *hungry*

at times, never empty. There'd be *caprese* and *Who else'll have some,
come on, don't make me finish it all by myself.* He'd tell us
again about Italy, say *Next comes the primi,*

he'd have the *risotto* or *gnocchi*, the rest of us whatever, noodles
in red sauce, and after, keeping the cloth napkin tucked at his neck,
for him the *secondi*, veal, chicken, lobster…

we'd drag our forks through what was left on our plates. And he'd have
put in for several *contorni*, the parmesan-graced asparagus
plus a few more to pass around—we'd sample

these for his sake in our fullness. He'd never think we'd had enough,
though we'd be dazed by the time the *tiramisu* arrived, one
for each. He'd finish his, and at last lifting

the bib from his collar, would ask for the check. My father never said
what was the matter. He'd take his Alka-Seltzer and Tums
through the night, wind up in front of the TV

in the den before dawn, and head out in the dark for work. He never said
restless, but I watched his relentless thrashing in his hospice
bed—he wanted to get dressed and out

to the car, saying *Come on let's go get the soup. What are we waiting for?*
I wonder if that soup was his mother's winter borsht, roots
grounding us once more in Minsk

or Vilnius, but I'm convinced it was a rich *minestrone*. And evenings
I picture him driving alone in those sun-dried hills of his
heaven, to dine at the next stucco inn.

Jewish Cemetery Night

Those headstones at Mount Carmel, each
must weigh more than a man, and taken
a couple of men a piece to bring down,
one then the next, nearly a hundred,
into the night. This was a team,
I imagine—together they pressed
their shoulders and chests and cheeks
and palms in uncanny brief intimacies
into the names of women and men
who walked the Northeast Philly streets
before these raiders were born. I see
the impression of some part of *loving*
father remain for minutes embossed
in the pad of flesh under a thumb. Another's
brow is stamped with the Hebrew letter
aleph that stands for the first of the Ten
Commandments. I hear the men grunt
in unison on the heave after *three*.

And the gratification, the bonding
these guys, I'm sure they're young, must be
able to feel, with what they've achieved—
what lives have they been leading? Is this
as close to a shared heatedly held
meaning as they can get, faceless
amalgam of the dead under their feet
and available to be blamed? The hugs
these topplers must've exchanged, shined
by their sweat in the moonlight. What lives
led to this? That it was just common
hate could uplift them? Don't they drink
their pints after work in the tavern, cheer
and curse the game over the bar? Doesn't it
keep their hides secure round their hearts
and their eyes off each other? I think
it's that secret aloneness does it, down
in the dark dark as the dirt.

A Visit

This other light she's wrapped in
lifts the furrows life left in her
skin. All her ages now,

or none—no shadow where
she leans at something like a desk.
Her dark pen streams an ink-

black shine along the vein-blue
lines down one white page
then the next. The letters weave

like seaweed in a tide-swept river
mouth. Silent lips move
with her hand—a kind of speech.

I start to wake, to drift
between two lands. She couldn't
see me, and I couldn't read.

My Brother and I at Har Jehuda

The cemetery grounds go weedy and unmown,
the shared headstone sinking lower in the late-
summer growth. Below the engraved names
and dates, what's under BELOVED HUSBAND
on the left and BELOVED WIFE on the right
goes hidden for now in a splash of green blades
and stems of what, chicory, Queen Anne's lace,
yarrow, I don't know, and can't quite recreate
the phrases we worked out that are now carved
into those polished squares, for him something
about how he'd still light our way, and for her
how she'd danced through life, yes that's close,
but I'm looking past the rows and out through
the wire fence at the backs of those brick houses

where I can practically hear people hollering
just like our folks before they moved their bones
in under this overgrowth, how they'd fill up
a living room, bedroom, or kitchen with bitter
volleys, music we'd finish our homework to,
what they thought they were keeping low after
we'd gone to bed. I'd listen late as if studying
what to anticipate in love's name. We're awake
now and they're not. We're standing here quiet
enough to hear Darby Creek twenty yards west
and Township Line Road on the far side of those
houses. Some grass and blue flowers do seem
to lean in a swell on the granite with thoughtless
affection. I daydream the dead feel their peace.

II

THE NEWS AT GOLDEN GARDENS

And don't you feel also, perhaps, a stormy sorrow on the skin of time…

—from the poem "It Comes in Every Storm"
by Olga Orozco

While She's Angry

Now that I've up and opened
my window on this cold pink
autumn dawn, not much smoke
just now blown in from Oregon,

I can drink streams of sky
into my chest, syphon down
my whiffs of those wide heights,
and dream awake again

that you and I remain mingled
in our mother's breath, even
while she's angry with our fires,
even over all these miles.

CAN'T TELL YOU MUCH

In the frozen aisle's uniform glare
a tall boy stares. Not through the glass
doors at tubs of ice cream or the stacked
pizzas in cardboard. Through the air
ahead, toward the checkout registers,

but I'm sure it's nothing there, not the movie
magazines, racks of chocolate bars, dyed
carnation bouquets. I'd say he looks
amazed by a scene in the near future.

Come to a standstill as if he means
to keep what distance he can between
himself and his premonition, he's focused

not dazed. Oh, maybe he's stopped
his medication, or has he just
solved the geometry problem the beautiful
Miss Bulgari gave everyone yesterday,

or has he abruptly recalled
his father's final curse before
slamming the front door forever.... I dawdle,

couple yards off, convincing myself
some boxed organic broccoli florets
might ride away in my basket. I catch
the kid's waxen face. He's too transfixed

to notice my sidelong glances. I can't shake
the sense his vision is actual. I drive
home, eyes on the rainy road, his eyes

suspended before me, not swept aside
by the windshield wiper, not dispersed
by the passing headlights, and not later
dismissed by talk and kisses and dinner.

It persists in the present. He in his
untucked what is it green or blue shirt,
hair in a muss, I can't tell you
much, but his stare's fixed in my night
on what, a fireball, a fresh crater—

No Hope Makes a Missile

My sleeplessness at this distance
mails a donation of nothing to Kyiv.

My sped-up heart runs me closer
to no Russian's gun barrel. I divert

no bullet's path. And no prayer
of mine spares an old man by a window.

No hope makes a missile plough
into a field not a hospital. And neither

one of my hands flies from this night
into that choked daylight to coax

a shellshocked defender's finger
to finish squeezing a trigger. No

curse out of anger's lake, no matter
my rage's black leathery wings

and flaming breath, crisps a conscript
lured from Novosibirsk or Irkutsk.

At my age, still wishing my wishes
could kill or save! Could throw a rope

out of care's coil to one instant
orphan in that storming of fools.

To one child who'll know, soul's eye
catching the line as it falls

out of the haze. To take hold.
Don't let go now. Don't let go.

THE WIRE SAID

"…we have been most ourselves, when we have opened our doors…"
—Amy Davidson, in *The New Yorker*

Held up behind a red in evening rain,
my FM station on, I heard a man
who'd left his house in rubble, crossed a plain
and then a sea, gone north without a plan,
now faced a razor wire fence—it met
horizon at both ends. The wire said
a vast estate of folk more fortunate
had spread this far, and that its forbears bled
a sea to claim it. Then a rush of surf
it seemed poured through the radio—a gust
blown here, I thought, across the bordered turf,
from where the nomad shifted in the dust.
His ragged English rode like froth on flood.
It floated through the wire, blood to blood.

American Border Study: Two Bodies in a River

Oscar Alberto Martinez Ramirez and his daughter, Valeria,
Rio Grande, Matamoros, Mexico, June 24, 2019

We'll recall her small arm on his neck.
We'll forget them there in the shallows.

We wonder at the black cloth they share.
We don't get it was how he held her.

We see clearly her short red pants.
We miss the pink disposable diaper.

We note the bamboo stalks on the shore.
We grow our bamboo along the link fence.

We see sun in the river's slow ripples.
We have no fierce current here in the frame.

We're touched their dark heads wind up together.
We are spared their still-eyed stare.

We're shocked the camera shot them in the back.
We're not especially surprised.

We're living the lives they might have.
We haven't been breathing water.

We understand it's father and daughter.
We don't have our noses in the mud.

This Day

The Earth's held this house close
and brought it round out of the dark.

This chest remembers to widen
again—in pours the good air.

The heart still knows to take its own
share, and offers up the rest.

The blood, down its deltas, visits
the countless cells. The muscles are fed,

and on a wish for water they hinge
the limbs—the bones' ensemble stands,

out of its bed. By several footfalls
toward the faucet, it proves possible

to lower and turn the head,
part these lips at a small stream,

and receive this clean gift
of the rain needed to live. How

can I be the fountain of my fortune,
through all the smoke and confusion?

May my words find a current, this ink
hold fast to its leaf as it floats

to meet the prisoner, the gatekeeper,
wanderer camped at a wire fence,

kid who sleeps with the gun
his father left him. Luck is a demon.

How, this day, like water, like air,
can I enter your life? I can't see your face,

I don't have your name. I don't know
your despair. And this is our house.

Cholera Etude

Vast blue sky. Is it God's iris?
It stares at the camp in the dust.

A liter of saline's cost rises
to the demand. Bag of sorghum?

Gallon of clean water? Always
a delivery charge. Do you wish

to make a donation in rainclouds?
Enter your card number here. Type

prayers in this space, then upload.
There has been a surge in requests.

Responses are slowed. Deliverance,
near as breath, remote as the stars,

depends on invisible forces. Tents,
made of hand-dyed garments tied

to the staked limbs of dead trees,
shade wasted mothers and young.

The sky's blind as the barrel-end
eyes of the lost husbands' guns.

The News at Golden Gardens

Osaka's doctors have run low
        on the propofol to sedate
the breathless they must intubate.

                    *

        Turtles repose on the pond's logs
though it isn't sunny. A duckling
        scuttles over the planked walkway.

                    *

In Maharashtra, surgeons take black-
        fungus-colonized eyes from those
who otherwise will die.

                    *

        Today the tide's risen close
enough to reach the nearest
        of the ghost-pier's bleached posts.

                    *

Where, ever, isn't here? In Gaza,
        how will the bone-shaken rise
from their new era of stones?

                    *

        And here, on a taken inland
sea and its land, crows slash the wind,
        hawks hold drifts above the trees,

                    *

and a freight train groans in
        from south to somewhere, lugging,
God knows, what they need there.

Learning to Hold

must've begun in the supple and firm pod where the body formed, in that first
forever I'll never remember, and gone on in a fold of arms, welcome to the warm
milk, then to a song of coo and response—before the word, to belong.

Held rapt in the pulse and swell of the Cuban music my mama put on
to dance, and held in the suspense of my grandfather's bedtime tales, all along
learning. And, yes, held down if I wouldn't hold still for the shot, held

responsible in Mrs. McCurry's lens-magnified eyes for the scuffle I'd caused,
and held to the concrete anytime Elliott needed to prove he could pin me
again. All of these holds I've learned, and have, in my ways, passed along—

had my little brother to practice on, then my kids twisting in my grip. Given
my skills, I once slipped from the seize of two men a few steps from an ATM.
I've even pulled out of the magnetic field of a marriage, to my sad freedom.

Then there are holds I haven't been shown. Never cuffed. Never straight-jacketed,
nor shackled in a ship's hold, nor manacled to a portside post,
to be shown and sold. And I'm no Joseph left in a hole for purchaser pick-up.

Never a cramped freight car to a camp, to be kept and worked to the bone,
no bone-break baton in my ribs, no uniformed man's full weight pressing
my neck to the street. Oh I know gravity grounds us all in its democratic hold,

and time hauls our skeletons equally down through the orbits, till you and I mix
in the intimacy of our atoms dispersed, back in the compost of ends and origins,
while all the variations on human still burst to bloom through the womb-holds,

but I know, too, your heart's been squeezed harder than mine, your insides torn
by sheer rupture under the steel bow of the great trade vessel holding you
under, you with your other tongue, other part of town, other faith, color,

I don't know all the holds you've learned, I haven't climbed through your crushing
tunnel, but I have been learning to hold this hatch in my soul's hull open.
So you could lean over and unlatch yours, so the hurt-water pours.

A Prayer

A cormorant crosses a harbor low,
wings' pulse keeping an air pillow
on the bird's shadow, that black
belly a steady few inches aloft.

I know a soft blaze glows
in that dark fuselage. Fine fire courses
a delicate wire web to maintain
the arcane mechanics of constant

lift. A nameless attunement
in that sleek breast resets the ratio
heartbeat to wingbeat, pump's clap
matching the instant's requirement.

That fire's quiet, discrete. We spread
our flame out in whatever gods' name.
Our heat breaches containment.
We spark the wind with bright sticks.

I watch from an edge of the land
we've lit. I see the cormorant
reach a buoy and stand, wings held
wide to the air, a trusting, a prayer.

Meditation Inspired by James Baldwin
While Waiting to Board Delta Flight 1960

The stranger who flies in on a forged passport
might in some future moment riddle
my skin with the lead of his hate. Let there be
no argument. He might cross a border
river, crawl through a tunnel at night,
or drive across Broad Street the mile between
the house he grew up in and my shopping mall.
He might line up with me in the morning
to board the same bus for work. It is he
who also waits at Gate C-18
for my flight to LA. What does the stranger
seated just feet to my right carry
in secret in that gray-and-white personal
item? I'm trying not to imagine, but
it can't be helped, as I keep my own secret
presence wrapped in the dark of the flesh
in the cage of my chest, a stranger who hides
inside all my life, the undocumented
guest of my breath, who knows how to cinch
the nerves to my heart in an instant, who grips
the stalk of my brain and tugs to remind me
again of the nowhere I come from, he threatens
again to expose me, my darkness, my forgery,
my assumed name in the counterfeit ink
of my borrowed tongue. This stranger comes
morning and night up the aortic pipe,
up toward awareness again while I watch
the TSA man with the odd little stamp
in his hand to affirm or not that I am
who I say, or the stranger, the terror, I am.

LOST CROSSING

—for Jakelin Amei Rosmery Caal Maquin

The girl crosses from city to forest,
hand in her father's. The girl crosses
the rivers, riding her father's shoulders.

She crosses the dark under stars
her father says are our ancestors
watching us. She crosses the valleys

where her dreams land her, calling out
for her father who's hidden off in the brush
where he crouches to gather them edible roots.

She crosses long stretches of hunger
and thirst, and her father tells her
it isn't much farther north. The water

they find to drink is the water they find.
They cross brown streams, narrow and cloudy
rivers, she tires, her father tugs her

along by the wrist, as firm as he must,
as gentle as he can be. She crosses
back and forth between wake and sleep

on her feet, crosses the last stretch of dust
before her father draws her under
the shadow of a tall barrier

and lets her slump, lets her fall
to her knees and she drifts, crosses deep
where her rising fever's wide blue river

runs in a silver haze toward the sea,
and she lets that river take her, before
her father or anyone sees she's not there

for the final heave, not there
when the agents seize her father

and her, not there in her limp limbs

nor behind her swimming eyes, won't ask
for the fresh water her blood's long-shrunken
rivers still need, and she slips

farther off from the sand of their perch
on those banks of the Promised Land.
She crosses into forever elsewhere,

father squeezing the air for her hand.

THE ONE WHO'S LEFT WATER

Someone's leaving water for you
in the last sandy stretch before you

reach Ajo, if you do. Same water
left on Earth for us by the luminous

icy-tailed comets. Same water
Moses struck loose from the rock.

Water of milk welled in the breast
for the naked new traveler pressed

from the first watery house
through the wet lips of genesis. I see

Jesus turning the creosote bushes
to clay vases full of the freshest

quaffs for the lightheaded weaving
wanderers north. And Mary's tears,

free of salt, spilled on the tongues
of the flaccid pallid little ones

in the arms of their parched bearers.
Some One leaves water for you

in a plastic jug as you come crossing
toward liberty or a cage.

You'll need this offering first
fallen from space filling your veins

when you meet the officers face
to face. And may the water-bearer

be not arrested, not detained,
nor convicted for such grace.

May the one who's left water walk
the Sonora back and forth,

as if there were no border.

43

Song Off the Water

—for Thomas Hubbard

Standing on the mud of the present edge of what we call Union Bay,
looking across to the burial ground *STITICI* known also as Foster Island,

I see the 520 Bridge pinned to the bay's silver skin. The span rises
farther out, over what goes by Lake Washington. And I can hear,

through near-windless air, droning off waters forgetting their *LUSHOOTSEED*
names, in the murmur of motors and tread-rumble, a chorus of time-

drowned throats—oh it's bay and lake as much as it's bridge, day's wet
atmosphere much as those chambered eruptions and spun wheels' whirring

on strutted-up road, or it's artifact of my cochleae blown by so much
rock'n'roll, or the acid I took having carved its cross-channels

in my brain's marshes—a chanting out of the platforms and pylons…yes
out of the bridge or through it and skimming the water, reaching my ears

fresh or caromed off Laurelhurst's walls, that groan of the haul, incessant
whine of the shafts and pistons, gnash of the gears, and picking up

those pings off the shells of turtles warming themselves on these logs
by the shore. Altogether, it's the choral appeal of who paddled and fished here

in western redcedar dugouts, joined, I'm sure, by who spiked the rails
that skirted the bay, and maybe by those who cry across time and the world

out of their stormed villages, say, my people in Kovno. Could be
a voice slips from every hut burned by a crown, and every cell, wire pen,

cattle car, shackle hold, bullet-holed tent or shack is permitted
its window of sound—that choir calls and I listen, but can't follow, no

more than I could my grandparents' spats, their mud-hamlet rants
ringing the house, that Litvak yap of their love uninterpretable as these

gulls' cackles, as the crows' mocks from the alders or that kingfisher's
swoop-rattle. So what to make of this song off the water, where longhouse

villages drummed and whispered ten thousand years, where lone souls
in Broncos and Cherokees stir up a hum out of the bridge? I hear a hymn

and dirge—for us, the lost's broadcast, into this air they can't touch.

45

Smithed on the Anvil

The shooter's got US Flag toothpicks poked in his eyes. He's got extra white
stars sewn over his ears, got black and red stripes like a seared rare steak

on his back, a posse of long-nailed pain-devils prying open his ribs to attack
his heart, it's gone on like this for years, and the great hate has entered him,

sealed itself in with a moisture-lock layer like Vaseline spread on his lungs,
seized the root of his tongue, reached up and squeezed the transmission stalks

between his retinas and what his brain sees, so he's stuck with his twisted vision,
the American warrior prophecy, illustrated by devotees of Stan Lee,

written like scrimshaw carved on the inside walls of his cranium, look at him,
he seethes in the roar of his own packed bone stadium, he believes

a version of doctrine cooked into him, the convergence of triumph and doom,
not unusual among human males, no stranger than a kid's cowboy heroes

firing into the tissues of Injuns or Japs or Krauts while their own skin ruptures
red spouts, that glorious finish, that getting the hate out, that rubbing it in

with instant lead fingertips making the point at a distance and evading all future
debate. The shooter was made for this, smithed on the anvil of eternal vigilance. He,

alloy of densest emptiness radio talk show righteousness mental ward lingo
satellite TV memes and blank memories, lifts the elongate metallic gift

he bought himself to his head, and now that he's settled up with the anonymous
stand-ins for family fresh-dead, blows an escape hatch through his own brow.

THROWING A BOWL

Awake again this quietest hour between midnight and dawn, seeing
by what light leaks out through the last dream's cracks, minutes

one ought not make lasting commitments, I order a potter's wheel
up from the dark. I slap down a lump of the clay of the rest of my life

on that disc like a fretful bet, thump, got my hands slipping wet, and I press
into the fast-turning mass, shaping.

                            Hunched close, I pour my shadow's hope/
sorrow mix over the clay, so before it's a bowl, it may sense….

Each hand's heel and palm under to lift, then one delves from the top
to open a dark in the dark, a belly or womb, like in the broad urn on the mantel
where we drop our gloves and keys.

                          Then, fingers and thumb at the rim drawing
an emptiness up, already the brine of my breath spills in, the new hollow brims
with a suspension swirling along with the spin,

                                and in it swim things
dream's acids and enzymes never digest. They have lived in my chest, the rattles
and rings of door-slams circling now like little metallic fish in this cistern
of liquid air.

        Cold cringes and sweats, sawtoothed silences, gut punches, must I
go into the when and where? A backwash, my lungs' sloshing recesses into this
tidepool I widen and deepen with my heart's hands.

                              Tangles of deadheaded
stems, strips of tough plastic lasting long after the last of the gifts
they've wrapped,

                clicks of landline hang-ups like locks tumbling to seal off
lives, strangled wishes that somehow keep gasping, I fill the bowl's rising
welcome with more, each exhalation

                           a vouchsafing. My mother's finger
waving my way to indict the kid she must see in a mirror behind me,
snippets of my father's full-color

        cartoon American vistas, crinkled-up
five-and-dime photo-booth pics of the Bar Mitzvah kid with hair swept
John Lennon-like by a shoplifted comb,
        the torn pages of my underground
life in another language with my other wife, a map's squarish fragments
come apart along creases of fold as I've tucked it five thousand times
under the cardiac pipes—

      all my dreams find too much to hold.

I might sleep for another hour or two, beneath the unbreakable sky
as it moves over the world's ever-shattering news, front lines, plagues,
drowning islands and all, if

      the bowl's clay will only set, let me
wash my hands of it till light.

A Late Note

Maybe it was the walk we'd take
from where you'd park on Lancaster
Road, that block or so and around
the corner under the Rexall sign
onto City Line and a few doors more
to Mel's, his red white and blue
helical stripes writhing alive
in their wide cylinder out front, before
we'd even enter the shop's infinity
of mirrors, its mixed scents
of disinfectants and human sheddings;

that quiet stroll, or possibly also
the quick waggle and roll of the comb
and scissors in Mel's hands, cranky
lilt in the thick of his Polish shtetl
accent chatting with you as you'd stand
and check his work, as if it had to
be that good, and under the snips
my blinking back and forth between
our endless iterations behind the glass
and Mel's left forearm's blue numbers
half-escaping his white sleeve;

it might as easily have been you saying
nothing of where Mel had once lived
or what he'd seen, nothing before
our entry rang the bell over the door,
or while my hair fell on the pale sheet
cinched at my neck, or after
we'd left, getting back to the black
Buick, my scalp again feeling
the wind it had forgotten—maybe
all that was the frame, and what
you never would say was in it.

On a Day of Remembrance

International Holocaust Remembrance Day, January 27, 2022

Let's remember how they thought
they were finally cleaning things up.
Taking care of the rodent problem.

Not strange. The same way
we had the man spray downstairs
when moths had invaded the carpet.

You know how your scalp will itch
when you hear there are lice. Let's
remember this, inheritance meant

to make our skin crawl at the chance
of a spider, a scorpion, ants.
Older than ancient. Ancestral.

Remembrance? Let it spread across
every checkpoint and wired wall.
Let it stay all our swatting hands.

After the Missile Strike on the Train Station in Kramatorsk

I try to imagine the instant
rupture of steel concrete flesh,
crowd on a platform in a distant
town I can't pronounce—how is it
this sets loose a memory? I've never been
shockwaved deaf, blast-snapped a bone,
bled out on the ground or inside.

In my click-window, the row of black
bags. No more of those lives. Still,

I'm four or five, my mother
and Aunt Reba either side of me under
the highest ceiling ever in the vastest
room in the world. They each hold
one of my hands, tug me along
in a hurry to board. A great voice echoes
our platform number.

Our Own Thievery

The bed squealed on us to the shadows
of our getaway. We whispered, laughed,
and let the daylight's inquest go on
delivering its indictments to the trees,

the rooftops, the glass towers, tent-dwellers
working the ramps, all the bright hulls
drifting the blacktop canals—the sun's
floodlight on the easy evidence, while we lay

low in our cove. Sure, we noticed
the curtains, shifty in the open window.
And we overheard that soft flip-flop
testimony of the fabric on frame and sash.

Hints of wind reached in like the murmurs
of a courthouse crowd. The air knew
where to find us. But why now do I spin it
this way? We'd made off with the timeless

gem of an hour, till the light fell
and a chill slipped in. We were even granted
a sweet release, and when we walked
from each other after, it felt like free will.

So, let the record show we'd done nothing—
nothing, though while entangled together
we'd heard the volcanic dad two doors down
erupting again—we'd gone on

teasing sighs and moans and simple words
from each other. Had we registered
any of those sirens that keep calling
out of the University District? We hadn't

thought the loose fence slat's slaps could be
gunfire down there. Well, look at us,
in no way impaired, just heartsick
with our own thievery—we stole the day,

licking the light off each other's shoulders.
We'd siphon the stars down our throats.

53

III

LASTNESS

The sea

seemingly a constant to the naked eye is one
long goodbye…

—from the poem "Bronzed"
by Dean Young

LAST PADDLE

By the old gasworks north end of the lake,
we poked into a shady lagoon shaped
by a row of houseboats and an alder-lined bank.

The graffiti'd-over signs warned us
don't try to wade or swim, the sediment
dangerous. There were some kids

playing waist-deep where a path led in
off a homeless camp in the trees. We saw
the lakeshore road we'd come in on, its gravel strip

home to a long stretch of trailers and vans,
a new neighborhood of the disbelonged. We hid
from the wind and boat-wake for a while

in our glassy-skinned alcove. Swallows
snatched insects from the quiet air.
A brown duck, bill in the water, snacked

behind a loose curtain of leaves and catkins.
We drifted. A dark dragonfly slowed
the seconds as it crossed between

our little boats. It was a measureless moment
of this bright day as our world went on
fraying. Then we pulled on water, away.

Poem for My Country

Not far from my city, I walked under tall trees
by a river whose name soon escaped me.

Silty-green eddies, white froth dressing
the rocks, flat current over what I thought

must be the depths, a riffle dazzled
the shallows. I lost perspective

to the strobe of the wind-shaken maples'
foliage fringing the shore. Were they swallows

who sped and veered, who caught the living
dust of the hovering bug constellations?

A few splashes some yards upriver,
little eruptions of silver, what might be

a fish, I bent for a better look under
a branch, and saw on the edge up ahead

a kid spin a flat rock to skip, and it did.
What country is this? A moment in wonder,

no answer. The water coursed past
in and out of the bright and the dark, I heard

the elements' vigorous frictions, dignified
groans of the cedars and firs, and imagined

the current grinding away at the stones.
What country is this? Perhaps it is known

to the singing boughs spread over the banks,
to the stones, or the invisible fish.

TERRIFIED TREMOLO HYMN

The April morning slept on in the shade of rain, the light as if through
a tent's cloth. I remember, around noon, still yawning. Then the clouds

pulled up their stakes in time for the wind, whose great body drove in
like a drunk evangelist in a finned Cadillac—wind like a spiritual rant
in the branches, pale young leaves and the plum blossoms shaking mad

in their sudden devotion, manic in the gospel of beams. I stood under
an order of crows who'd broken their vows to surf the fast curls of the air.

A dog chained to a post barked at a rustling bush. A girl on her lawn ran
in circles and screamed, her voice sailing off east on her thrill's wings.

The blow pressed tears from my eyes, and in the blur something came clear.
This twisting of arms, ferocious caress, urgency grabbing any who stood in it
hard by the shoulders, by the boughs, wings—if time has its hands on us,

it had me good in that wind, like a mob's brutes showing up for a shakedown.
I knew I was late paying off on breath's promise, way past the grace

period. This was the wake-up, time's fist in the gut, so I'd get whose oxygen
was it being knocked out of me. It's then the wind ripped my hat off, sent it
skidding the street—like a kid chasing a ball I ran after that beast on the asphalt

and might've got hit had a car turned the corner. Wind wilding my hair, I panted
hard to catch up, and tugging my hat back on snug, for more than an instant,

I was sure in that low roar I heard the calls of my dead warning me from where
they swam in the wind-flood—no I'm not making this fit some religion, not
one more afterlife myth for pimping young fools to war. Call it delirium.

Say I was lightheaded after that sprint. But look, the plum petals were being torn
loose and thrown out on the air in broad waves, a great shimmer of sunlight
and shadow, a mass migration of weightless tumbling ghosts. I walked

into that wind, gripping my brim, shuddering like the old X-15 rocket plane
crossing the sound barrier, bolts and seams threatening rupture under

the siege of such speed. I felt all my small pieces shiver in my thin sheath—
I was blown-through, lit-through, and saw I was made of such tiny flaps
as what flashed all around me. *Wind*, I thought—or did I sputter it out

loud—give me your old-time revival pollen-and-seed song. Awe me on back
to dust, to life, to form after form—I'll sing you my terrified tremolo hymn.

THAT SUMMERY LOOK

Early this morning, asleep, I was back
   in that living room. Dad at the hearth,
an elbow up on the mantel, drink
   in his other hand, we were discussing
his death, which was on its way.

I was admiring his pale blue suit,
   its easy-yet-tailored fit,
open-collar white shirt, tan loafers
   he wore without socks, that summery look
he went for. And his hair's walnut sheen,

its subtle wave, soft glow of his cheeks—
   here he was, the timeless guy
everyone liked. But we knew
   he was ill. I said *days to weeks.*
He answered quietly, *moments now.*

None of the steroid bloating, weakness,
   delirium, bedsores, stumbling speech.
And no denial. No last-minute deals.
   Helping me with it this time. Able
to settle for what had been possible.

I reached my hand out to stroke
   his jacket sleeve, to feel the material,
try to tell if it was linen, cotton,
   silk, or a blend. It is what seemed
to matter, still, this close to the end.

No holding a straw to cracked lips,
   no watching him choke on his pills.
My chance to see the man leave
   as he'd lived—he would set down the glass,
grasp me by the shoulders and peer

into my eyes for a while, then look
   past me once he'd spotted the taxi
through a front window. He would let go
   and head for the door. But I woke
just as I touched the blue sky he wore.

The Humility of Old Men

might gout a big toe might turn
an ankle whose ligament got loosed up
years ago under a basket

                                        might wear
through the cartilage of a right knee

on its way to a hip's ball
                                    and socket
and on from there

                         it'll flaccid
the groin's passion gear find a pocket
of bowel to inflame

                          it will infiltrate
the diaphragm and make camp in the heart

tighten the arteries stiffen the lungs
and steepen the hills

                          it will ascend
and drill itself into the pulp of teeth

pull down the shoulders brittle the neck
cloud the eyes yellow the world
                                      humility

shrinks old men sometimes to a ripeness
a friends-with-death kind of translucence

lets us see the well-traveled child
who smiles at me from his hospital bed

Unveiling

My brother and I idle by the plot. I spot our mother
stirring the rolled oats again in the light of the old kitchen
window. She coughs, still clearing her chest of the smoke

she welcomed into her lungs last night. Smog's gathered
around her heart. She's dying, I know, to cry a loud
curse, but we are her new life on our twin stools

at the wooden counter, our hungry bowls before us
like alms cups, and if she can't swallow her dark flares
and feed us, fear is she'll become what she hates

of this long dry valley she's traveled, coal hills to city
to city, her father long dead of a curse in his bowels,
her husband out there in the beams of the day's adulations,

her mother a full day away by train and decreeing
the distance calls for *No tears* on the phone—I blink
into our new polished window of stone as she strikes

the rim of the pot again with the neck of that spoon,
the lean winter light on her yellow terrycloth robe
like the thin glow of a new season. I listen—the tin-drum

repeat through the white steel of the stove the unsettled
question of weeping's welcome, then through the dark
grating of her carved name, I hear the spoon scraping.

Talk at the End of Summer

All my three offspring in town for the last
of August, we potluck into the dusk
on the weathered deck, big Japanese maple
leaning its reddened breeze-shivered leaves
and samaras over us as if to eavesdrop.

Low in the plum-purple southeast, Saturn
grants us an audience. The kids, grown
and partnered, talk of not having kids—no
little round mouths irresistibly calling
for more rice or milk than there is, no new
throats in the drought, and no pink lungs
panting for oxygen while it runs out.

I see the loose ends of my lineage, bloomless
stems, sprouts swept useless across clay
hardpan—our uncanny design gone
fruitless. There won't be a miracle
miniature hand come to clutch my thumb, no
pair of womb-fresh wide eyes ushering
a jaundiced old one back into love's home.

So let it be these young, whose genes
have swum eons on a rough tide of births
wanted and not. Let Saturn see these
thoughtful ones, faces dusky as the rose
petals fallen along the fence, eyes casting
moon-like light before moonrise, lips
reposed between soft-spoken reflections….

Let my awe show as these once little ones
discuss the loss of their intricate code.
Will Saturn bless them? Can these dangling
seed-wings hear? Does anything earthly
remember? I'm kissing each child goodnight.

WHAT WAS THE QUEEN ANNE'S LACE

October's entered wearing a scent,
a blend of wood smoke, hint of late rose
and tattered lavender, that burnt-latex

aroma left when a kid's peeled off after
slamming the door, rain-damp tobacco
smolder, fresh rot of fallen apples—

she must hope we'll at least nod to her
if not bow, not just turn to another
calendar picture of autumn's gold aspens,

not simply gearshift the nerves to type 10
for the month. To not fall for the name
but into the body and breath, the long light

playing the wakes of ducks on the pond
between the stadium and the lake. To stop
and honor the battered heads of the rushes.

To look out across the landfill flats,
sundown rust on the countless brown cones
of what was the Queen Anne's lace, ragged

and leaning together like spent exiles
right where they've thrived. They're brittle
and quietly click in the gusts. October,

camp where a vanished moon will return
to bless the wind-shaken twigs, here,
where summer'd spread a sharp pennyroyal

odor around the pond's rim, I draw in
hard through the nostrils, the summer spell
gone. All the young ducks are grown

and proud in their squabbles. Here she is,
October or Winterfylleth or god knows
what to call her. My shoes in her mud,

I'm half-wishing October were somebody
else. I'm part back before the smoke,
before September's drop ceiling of ash,

and part drawn to a new month's perfume,
lingering char in the air, whiff of muck,
mix of spores, ozone of the imminent

storm, fragrance of worms, and the notes
my nose can't detect, a Coho somewhere
nearby in an osprey's grip, close

as a coyote must be seizing a rabbit
from under the dusk-umber cover of wild
carrot. October stretches before me,

the brush turns velvet, and I breathe her
incense of reckon and loss into my own
slow wreck of muscle and bone. October,

what are we to lay to rest? I hear a siren
crossing the lake bridge. I inhale first
leaf-dust—I'm lost in your ocher dress.

LASTNESS

Time I confess, right here, under
the branches of this naked katsura,
its malty death scent in the air—

now while I'm surrounded by evidence
I couldn't help it. Not this autumn,
the Japanese maple in its fatal flare,

freeway's blue roar a mournful rage,
allure of pure formlessness in the haze….
I mouth a word for it all that isn't quite

right—too bitter and I want to spit
and I wince to picture my grimacing
listener who isn't anyone yet.

And will anyone imagine this planet
a woman whose typhoon whisper starts
in her throat the magma conduits?

And her lips all the parts that can touch
other parts—raindrops and bullets,
gale-blasts against breakwaters, worn

fingernails scratching at walls? She
also isn't coming up with the right
word. But as the sea's storms'

great speaker cones wail, the fires'
crests crescendo over the foothill
developments, the gunrunners run

our young into the ground, the bees
cease in the dirt, the orcas go bony,
and knowing the white bear drowns—

I admit to it. Even these brown leaves
crinkling in swells at my feet
now chime like the highest bells

and radiate their unsealed brilliance.
What's a word for this, world shining
her first face through life's dying?

THE WANTING

The wanting, I felt I saw in the dark
brown beetle working its way toward the shining
eye of the good size rabbit dead
on its side by the trail, the wanting

in how that tiny-legged disc of an insect
climbed through what for it was the rough
heath of the rabbit's cheek, the wanting

gone only hours out of the rabbit,
its stillness off its feet and its tolerance
for the bug any live paw would bat at
my evidence for that fresh lack of wanting,

coat still smooth, unnamable color
of the earth's cover of dead leaf mulch
the rabbit must've been suited for, wanting

its life as a body, as my body wants
mine, as the little live coin
of the beetle moved just a thumbnail's width
in the moment I watched—it must be one wanting

life, the sheen-shielded beetle, the legless pale
feasters sure to inch in by the night,
the child I was at the milk of my wanting

I sucked and sucked in the unbroken
weaving of mothers and fathers, all the way
back to the sun-simmered broth of life—
I thought, the hunting, the blades, the wanting

to kill anything to eat and breathe, must be
inseparable from our love, and I lifted
my eyes, past the trees, to the road's drumming.

Study by Window Light

I won't say beauty, so you won't think
I mean the last of your youth. I don't
need to see some peachy face beaming
original trust, wide eyes blinking
up at a cloud-puff creature parade.

I don't much like that dusky tarnish
brushed onto the lids to emphasize
innocence with a bruised look. If ever
I wished to rescue, harbor, or transport
a poor pseudo-you, I don't now.

I do need those lines years facing
the light have drawn from your eyes'
corners. I need the blue veins' tint
on your temples' plains, and to settle
my shreds in the gullies east and west
of your brave complicated lips.

There's respite in the long creases
time and mothering's given your breasts.
Here's a land where the air is alive
with listening. Your traveled hand rests
on this wanderer's wind-burned hide.

Here's a sky whose cumuli come down
around me like knowing limbs, a voice
like yours in the vapor, an understanding
closer than speech. I won't say beauty—

unless we can reclaim the contraband
held in that name, steal it from the gloss
cases of the magazine pages,
set the actual free where the word's been
lashed with millions of miles of eyeliner

down to the skin-and-bone runway flash
behind the screens—beauty as broken
code, the harnessing of so much human
need to be seen. I won't say beauty—
till we've brought it home to our kitchen

stove, table, our weeks' old rose
petals like little red lifeboats left
adrift near the salt, in evidence gravity's
excellent work on your bent shoulders
and my paunch, this raggedy nurture
we manage, leaning together

into our undoing. This dim winter
day, cold by the window, you huddle
wrapped in the woolen throw. The light
infuses frayed strands of your hair,

matching the soft sheen of the naked
alder out there. Your cheek's a mottled
field of purples and earths, its furrows
a text to erode unread. I won't say
beauty, but touch what'll go unsaid.

Pain Syndrome

You can open an account in a shoulder
or hip, in one side of your neck,
or sure, your low back—but you won't know

till it's chosen. Then, it's just a matter
of making deposits, which you can deduct
from what you owe the world. Look,

it's a pretty good deal. There's a tear
in your cartilage, tendon, ligament, maybe
the spine's slow collapse crushes a nerve—

you send checks to that address, compounding
your bitter riches, as if to thicken
your inland sea's sediment floor

with that grit of breakdown, failure's bone-
powder, holdings come to far greater than
any specialist's arthroscope can

explore. Then let the instruments poke
into your hurt's glowing red
star of a joint capsule. Take whatever

rays they focus to audit that fissure
filled with your pain's layered ore. They might
gain purchase by increments, but never see

all you've accrued. And the bell rings
closing your day while it's still bright
as a morning in childhood. It's been a fight,

a war, and you didn't start it. You had to
strain against gravity. Your nature made you
haul that child, elder, loved one

or stranger, over the dry hills
and through the mud valley, remember?
It was the world that tore you.

Blues for the Fathers

The fathers keep on disappearing
into the sun. Every morning
a father flies east. In the afternoon
one'll drive west.

        And midday,
look at the man bend at his knees
to kiss a girl's cheek then rise
to ride invisible escalators
up the floors of the sky.

        In the night
another steps out and tries on his metal
wings in the driveway—tin or something
hammered to such a thinness he lifts,
tilting toward sunrise.

        Look at that
father open a letter at breakfast,
then careful to miss everyone's eyes,
push back his chair and let the light
swallow him at the door.

        You've seen
the one who pours himself more of that
clear drink till he sees right
through you, into a bright-in-the-dark
that's not the sun.

        And a father comes
home from a journey, hospital, war…
only to disappear out a window,
leaving his heart still chugging
in its fuselage.

        Yes, you know—
though moving closer was hard,
and arms that once held you never rose,
you leaned over, set your ear
to that burned hull, and heard.

Before Gone Can Be Believed

They can't all be ready to enter the light
right away. The slight girl will keep running
down the demolished street toward her building
that like herself has just lost its shadow,

the tower of apartments now looking like sky smoke
and cloud—so intent is she on falling
into her grandmother's arms she can't yet

notice her own weightlessness, nor that she steps
through the collapsed beams. It's like phantom
limb syndrome, but of the whole self gone
before gone can be believed. A father flies

toward Kyiv on a swift current of worried love,
sure it's alright to head home as the fight's gone dead
silent, not sure how he speeds fleet

as Hermes, not the least bit out of breath—
he's filled with the world-breath he moves through.
And the Russian kid who's just bled out, guts
on his lap in the truck, has opened the door and gone

looking for who'll tell him what this war is
about. Or give him the time of day. He feels
as unseen as before he was born. Maybe

it'll be the old woman after all, hovering
like a swarm of fine cake flour in the 14th floor's
afterglow, who's ready first, who'll shuffle in those
fake-fur slippers—skimming the static

electricity's little shocks up off the wall-to-wall
carpet like at our grandmother's—down the hall
hung with love's portraits, leading into the bright.

Blood Water Light

in my grandfather's eyes blinking away
at the dust stirred off the shelves of Ralph's
Army Navy on Market in Wilmington—

mites and specks of lead, tiny paint flecks
and shreds of cardboard, invisible
wisps of the twine he's tied around boxes,
orphan bits of pine left by the saws…all

riding along on his lids' reddened edges
and caught in the wet of that blue-veined shine
the whole way home on the train. He rubs

the heels of his hands into those sockets
and thinks only *tired.* He climbs the long stairs,
enters the echoes of 30th Street Station's
grand concourse, and exits close under

the tall wings of a bronze Archangel Michael
lifting a soldier from the world. He finds
his tailfinned Dodge in its film of Philadelphia

grime, and drives to 60th & Cedar
for a late dinner of left-over fish
in the kitchen. He lights a drugstore cigar,
sips instant decaf my grandmother brings him,

and drags ashen smoke like more dust
down his windpipe just like the doc says *don't
it'll kill you one night.* Tonight I'm looking

into the blood water light of his dust-
scoured eyes, into that huffing torrent of his
love's effort, that rude spitting immigrant
thick-hearted oxygen-thirsty current

of him, who churns through the dust
for us toward the shore till breath gives out
ahead where that gleaming surf scrubs.

Offering

It'll be *someone*, an evening you're more than half-
gone with loss, gone enough you can hear
the cottonwoods' judgments, and the crow crowd's
jeers from the alders, until *someone* comes.

Before you even notice, *someone* sits down
and faces you, knees almost touching yours,
you feel that interstellar remoteness
and intimate presence at once—it starts

the fragments shaking loose. All the pieces
you've felt stabbing at your insides, they rise
out your mouth, slip from the brims of your eyes, fall
like shining crumbs of glass from your ears

in the slant light. That face, familiar but whose? It's
someone who reads your brokenness, who's heard
the shatter-bits grinding, sniffed the silicate
dust that's wafted out of your lungs.

Between you and *someone* the glittering shrapnel
seems to melt. Was it ice? *Someone* offers
water cupped in joined palms. You'll drink.
Not bitter not sweet, you inhale a hint

of cold mineral creek-bottom, of that granite-bed
brook where you hunted newts as a kid.
And as you breathe deeper, as if you're back
kneeling in maple leaf shade in that gully's mud

behind the brick houses, you look up
at what must be the tint of dusk that's always
settling on us. *Someone*'s gone. Sunset's own wings
open to the edge of the world. You'll go on.

Rhythm of Light

Not till this last stretch, crick
in the neck, grind in the left
hip, twinge right Achilles,

lungs too stiff to fill easy
and quick with all the breath
these hills demand. Not till this

raft of nights, dark grinning
like a lamp through the roof.
And the leg veins' valves fail,

by each day's end to my shins
in marsh like the alders swamped
in their autumn ponds. Sure now

a wind'll come fell me, I begin
letting love in. Just as I start
my drowning. Gurgle and cough

mornings on the bog trail
out of dream. Seems I'll float
where I fall, won't be so cold

as I thought. The rhythm of light
on the ripples, turns out is you
leaning over the bed to stroke

my arm with two fingers. No,
not until now, this old
throat's groans like the gusts

bending the groves' bones,
so like returning, this
close to the first waters, you

These Night Visits

I know it's desire's horsehair
brush that applies pale wash
and paints the dark with what

I wish, shadowless and vivid
image, you. You are back
it seems, and looking silvery

by a psyche's light. Close
and in exquisite focus, each
fine eyebrow hair right

where it likes to be. I am in
your company, best the nights
the fewest photons can slip in

past the blinds—no moon
or stars, and my want's own
brightness has its chance,

I'm seeing you with my eyes
open. I won't push this
fortune. No I'll warn myself,

don't lean in with these lips or
dare extend a hand. I know
your face floats on the water

of the dark. I breathe slow
to keep you. A flash out there,
you're gone. But not nowhere.

COUNTRY MUSIC

I'd stand on a flat rock low to the river,
cast over the eddies, drop the lure
into fast water, reel to keep the hook
off the bottom, and feel for a strike.

Up there out of the buzz of my city
Sundays—where the Sultan runs
under twin bridges, railway and Route 2,
to join the Skykomish—I'd hear the deep

drone of the mountain runoff's tons
gushing over the stones, that incessant
crash on the riverbed's hidden ridges,
the high tones broadcast off the crests

fringed with foam, that churn working
oxygen down to the fish. It was often
the kids came with. One autumn
the older hauled in a Coho. I remember it

flipping itself, sides red as the vine maple
spread on the opposite shore, one eye
after the other on blank blue sky
till the boy conked it. That shudder

we'd seen before, a few seconds,
and it was no trouble to pull the hook.
With or without a catch, we would roll
back with our blood full of that country

music, that rush in our veins,
the shiver of snowmelt in our spines.
Sometimes I'd hear a dull knock
from below—the river turning a rock.

Continuous

I give the emptiness in my chest to the sky,
sparks in my head to the night, although
I earmark the light in my eyes for the sand
of bay floors where the flounders live.
May my bones' tiny archways coalesce
in the cool tunnels dug under border walls.
I donate the wishes caught in my throat
to the tongues of kids on hot streets. Songs
in orbit around my heart should be flung
360 to seed the musings of tent-dwellers
alongside the freeways. I send my longings
to fluff up the froth in the heads of beers
in the nowhere-from-here taverns. I offer
my summers' joys to clear the airways
of little allergic and asthmatic coughers.
Let my horrors add shine to the spiderwebs
toddlers and cats find under end tables.
And may all my spaces return to continuous
with the full breadth of the world. The rest,
the atoms, can play life or dust as they will.

GRATITUDE

The creation of this book of poems would not have been possible but for the faithful presence and encouragement of many around me, named here and not. Jill McCabe Johnson and Tina Schumann, both of Wandering Aengus Press, have been essential to the completion and refinement of the manuscript—I cherish their affirmation of this collection. My closest allies in the development of this work have been fellow writer Alina Rios (whose terribly keen ear and eye have been crucial in the shaping of many of these poems) and my brother Ford Myers (on whose intimate appreciation of much personal backdrop I've consistently relied). I'm grateful to the members of my regular poetry consultation group, to the poets and fine listeners who attend Seattle's Easy Speak gatherings, to poet and fellow *Bracken* editor Kate Deimling for her sensitive manuscript review, to Charlene Breedlove for all her support during and after her time as Poetry Editor at *JAMA*, and to Donald Hall for his impassioned emphasis on the music as we corresponded shortly before his death. There are, in truth, many others as well, whom I thank now and always. The world writes the poems, *through* us. ~JM

ACKNOWLEDGMENTS

My ongoing thanks to the editors of the publications noted below, in which the following poems first appeared:

"Word of Our Crossing"—*Rise Up Review*
"Her Winter Borscht"—*RHINO*
"Rain's Memory"—*The Shore*
"Name I've Never Heard"—*Passager*
"Gavel"—*HOLE IN THE HEAD re:VIEW*
"A Piece of String"—*Terrain.org*
"Through the Blows"—*West Texas Literary Review*
"Sketch for a Counter-Manifesto"—*Naugatuck River Review*
"A Few Wars"—*On the Seawall*
"Having First Heard of the Ivory-Billed Woodpecker on its Being
        Pronounced Extinct"—*Split Rock Review*
"The Road West"—*Winning Writers*
"Empathy's Shadow"—*Southern Humanities Review*
"Nearing the After"—*Natural Bridge*
"I Picture Him Driving"—*National Poetry Competition Winners' Anthology
        2021* and *The Poetry Review* (The Poetry Society)
"Jewish Cemetery Night"—*Rattle*
"A Visit"—*The Coachella Review*
"My Brother and I at Har Jehuda"—*Bear Review*
"Can't Tell You Much"—*Zócalo Public Square*
"No Hope Makes a Missile"—*Wordpeace*
"The Wire Said"— *McLellan Poetry Winners 2016*
"American Border Study: Two Bodies in a River"—*Rattle*
"This Day"—*Crosswinds Poetry Journal*
"Cholera Etude"—*Cutthroat*
"The News at Golden Gardens"—*So we go about our days* (Winchester
        Poetry Festival winners' anthology 2021)
"Learning to Hold"—*Aesthetica*
"A Prayer"—*Parabola*
"Meditation Inspired by James Baldwin While Waiting to Board Delta
        Flight 1960"—*The National Poetry Review*
"Lost Crossing"—*Poets Reading the News*
"The One Who's Left Water"—*Tinderbox Poetry Journal*
"Smithed on the Anvil"—*The Tishman Review*
"Throwing a Bowl"—*Halfway Down the Stairs*

"A Late Note"—*Pittsburgh Poetry Journal*
"On a Day of Remembrance"—*Rattle*
"After the Missile Strike on the Train Station in Kramatorsk"—*Mason Street*
"Our Own Thievery"—*The Greensboro Review*
"Poem for My Country"—*The American Journal of Poetry*
"Terrified Tremolo Hymn"—*Ruminate*
"That Summery Look"—*On the Seawall*
"The Humility of Old Men"—*Another Chicago Magazine*
"Unveiling"—*Frontier Poetry*
"Talk at the End of Summer"—*Rust + Moth*
"What Was the Queen Anne's Lace"—*Atticus Review*
"Lastness"—*Southword*
"The Wanting"—*Ruminate*
"Study by Window Light"—*Slippery Elm*
"Pain Syndrome"—*Mason Street*
"Blues for the Fathers"—*Book of Matches*
"Before Gone Can Be Believed"—*The National Poetry Review*
"Blood Water Light"—*The Arcane Mechanics of Constant Lift* (chapbook, Sheila-Na-Gig Editions)
"Offering"—*The Arcane Mechanics of Constant Lift* (chapbook, Sheila-Na-Gig Editions)
"Rhythm of Light"—*Golden Handcuffs Review*
"These Night Visits"—*Golden Handcuffs Review*
"Country Music"—*The Night Heron Barks*
"Continuous"—*Innisfree Poetry Journal*

ABOUT THE AUTHOR

Jed Myers' prior books of poetry are *Watching the Perseids* (Sacramento Poetry Center Book Award, 2014) and *The Marriage of Space and Time* (MoonPath Press, 2019). His fifth and most recent chapbook is *The Arcane Mechanics of Constant Lift* (winner, Sheila-Na-Gig Chapbook Competition, 2022). His work has appeared in *Prairie Schooner, Southern Indian Review, Rattle, The Poetry Review, RHINO, The Greensboro Review, Rust + Moth, Terrain.org, On the Seawall, Solstice, Nimrod International Journal,* and elsewhere. Myers lives in Seattle, where he's a psychiatrist with a solo therapy practice and Clinical Professor at the University of Washington. He's Editor of the journal *Bracken. Learning to Hold* is his third full-length poetry collection and winner of the Wandering Aengus Press Editors' Award.

About the Press

Wandering Aengus Press and its imprint Trail to Table Press are dedicated to publishing works to enrich lives and make the world a better place.